MAP OF CAMEROON

Cameroon

———	International boundary
—·—·—	Province boundary
★	National capital
⊛	Province capital
+—+—+	Railroad
———	Road

0   50   100 Kilometers
0   50   100 Miles

Mercator Projection

NIGER

Lake Chad

Nguru

Makari

Fotokol

N'Djamena

Potiskum

Maiduguri

Kousseri

Bama

Waza

Kari

Mora

EXTRÊME-

Mokolo

Maroua

NORD

Bauchi

Gombe

Mubi

Bourrah

Yagoua

Bongor

CHAD

Guider

Kaélé

Jos

Figuil

Léré

Fianga

Lai

NIGERIA

Yola

Garoua

Pala

Lafia

Réservoir
de Lagdo

Moundou

Doba

Benue

N O R D

Poli

Tchollire

Jelingo

Mbé

Benoué

Vina

Toubaro

Baibokoum

Makurdi

Wukari

Bali

Tignère

Ngaoundéré

Meiganga

Ouham

Bea

NORD-

Wum

Nkambe

A D A M A O U A

Ngaoundal

Bazoum

Enugu

Kumbo

Bankim

Tibati

Réservoir
de Mbakou

Bouar

Ikom

Mbengwi

Bamenda

Foumban

Yoko

Garoua Boulai

Baboua

CENTRAL

Mamfe

Mbouda

Batoussam

C E N T R E

Lom

AFRICAN

SUD-

Dschang

OUEST

Bafia

REPUBLIC

OUEST

Bélabo

Bangangté

Nanga Eboko

Calabar

Nkongsamba

Bafia

Minta

Bertoua

Batouri

Berbérati

Mundemba

Sanaga

Gamboula

Kumba

Yabassi

Monatélé

E S T

Kribi

Ndélélé

Buea

LITTORAL

Sanaga

Yaoundé

Abong Mbang

Malabo

Douala

Monatele

Mfou

Akonolinga

Yokadouma

Luba

Edéa

Eséka

Nola

Isla de
Bioko

Mbalmayo

Lomié

EQUATORIAL
GUINEA

Mespado

Kribi

Ngoulémakong

S U D

Sangmélima

Djoum

*Bight of
Biafra*

Campo

Ebolowa

Dja

Moloundou

Santo
Antonio

Ambam

Bitam

Minvoul

Souanké

REPUBLIC OF
THE CONGO

SAO TOME AND PRINCIPE

Bata

Ebebiyin

Mongomo

Oyem

Ayna

Ouesso

Sangha

*Ilha do
Principe*

EQUATORIAL
GUINEA

GABON

Base 802575 (R02413) 7-98

A WELCOME LETTER

Greetings, prospective Peace Corps Volunteers!

On behalf of all of the Peace Corps family here in Cameroon, I wanted to take a moment to welcome you to Peace Corps/Cameroon. We recently celebrated 50 years of continuous service and more than 3,000 Volunteers since 1962. Although it's been here for a long time, Peace Corps/Cameroon has adapted and changed over the years. We are doing our best to focus our efforts where we can make the greatest difference, given the wonderful volunteers, like you, who come here.

Cameroon is a wonderful and complex country and society that has been going through many changes. It is referred to as "Africa in miniature" due to the variety of ethnic groups, religions, and geographic diversity. It is also a country in which two of 10 regions have English as their official language, and the other eight have French as the official language.

I am sure you, like volunteers who have served before you, will find your service challenging, rewarding, and life-changing, both for you and for the Cameroonians with whom you will live and work when you are here. Ultimately, your time with the Peace Corps will be an immeasurable investment in your professional and personal life.

Before your departure, I ask you to please reflect honestly on your sense of commitment and motivation to work in Cameroon. Carefully review this Welcome Book, the Peace Corps Volunteer Handbook, and your Volunteer assignment description to learn more about the country, your assignment, and the policies that guide us all. We ask you to come with an open mind, patience, and a sincere willingness to share in the hardships and simple joys of your new community. Serving in the Peace Corps requires an inordinate commitment to leave behind much of what we are accustomed to as Americans. This includes daily comforts associated with our standard of living, as well as possible cultural entrapments we may seek to shed. However, this also includes cherished social and political beliefs, civil liberties, and standards of safety we take for granted. Please take the discussions regarding clothing seriously: dressing in accordance with local professional standards is very important to being accepted in your work and community. Heed the messages regarding harassment and safety and security. Developing personal coping mechanisms and adopting a safe lifestyle are among the many challenges you will face as a Volunteer.

A Peace Corps Volunteer is considered a professional person who has accepted an invitation to undertake demanding work under difficult circumstances, and who has decided to contribute his/her time and skills on a voluntary basis. We welcome you and pledge to support you in this endeavor. Cameroonians in communities throughout the country await the opportunity to share their lives and aspirations with you.

With best regards,

Jacquelyn Geier Sesonga (RPCV Mali, 1988–1991)
Country Director

TABLE OF CONTENTS

CORE EXPECTATIONS
FOR PEACE CORPS VOLUNTEERS

In working toward fulfilling the Peace Corps Mission of promoting world peace and friendship, as a trainee and Volunteer, you are expected to:

1. Prepare your personal and professional life to make a commitment to serve abroad for a full term of 27 months

2. Commit to improving the quality of life of the people with whom you live and work; and, in doing so, share your skills, adapt them, and learn new skills as needed

3. Serve where the Peace Corps asks you to go, under conditions of hardship, if necessary, and with the flexibility needed for effective service

4. Recognize that your successful and sustainable development work is based on the local trust and confidence you build by living in, and respectfully integrating yourself into, your host community and culture

5. Recognize that you are responsible 24 hours a day, 7 days a week for your personal conduct and professional performance

6. Engage with host country partners in a spirit of cooperation, mutual learning, and respect

7. Work within the rules and regulations of the Peace Corps and the local and national laws of the country where you serve

8. Exercise judgment and personal responsibility to protect your health, safety, and well-being and that of others

9. Recognize that you will be perceived, in your host country and community, as a representative of the people, cultures, values, and traditions of the United States of America

10. Represent responsively the people, cultures, values, and traditions of your host country and community to people in the United States both during and following your service

PEACE CORPS/CAMEROON
HISTORY AND PROGRAMS

History of the Peace Corps in Cameroon

The Peace Corps entered Cameroon in 1962 with 20 Volunteers who served as math and science teachers. Peace Corps/Cameroon's program grew and diversified to include inland fisheries, credit union and cooperatives education, English, community forestry, health and sanitation, and community development. Since then, more than 3,200 Volunteers have served in Cameroon. Currently, there are five robust projects in Cameroon: education, community health, environment, community economic development and youth development. The common themes that run through all Peace Corps/Cameroon projects are impact, focus, counterpart involvement, Volunteer competence, and organizational professionalism. Through collaboration and good teamwork, the Peace Corps has made a difference in many aspects of life in Cameroon, one community at a time.

History and Future of Peace Corps Programming in Cameroon

Peace Corps programs directly respond to development priorities of the Cameroonian government. For example, the Community Health Project was recently redesigned to focus on maternal and child health and HIV/AIDS prevention and mitigation areas in order to assist Cameroon in its achievement of Millennium Development Goals.

Although Volunteers are placed throughout all 10 regions of Cameroon, not every project is represented in every region. Each project concentrates on a few of the regions to maximize Volunteer impact and effectiveness.

Regardless of program area, all PCVs in Cameroon are involved in HIV/AIDS education. As a Volunteer, you will confront the effects of HIV on a very personal level. Some Volunteers will regularly meet with HIV-positive people and work with individuals living with AIDS. Volunteers need to prepare themselves to embrace these relationships in a sensitive and positive manner. You will need to anticipate these situations and utilize supportive resources available throughout your training and service to maintain your own emotional strength so you can continue to be of service to your community.

COUNTRY OVERVIEW:
CAMEROON AT A GLANCE

History

Since the journey of Hannon the Carthaginian in the fifth century B.C. to Mount Cameroon, which he named the "Chariot of the Gods," the country's fortunes have been subject to many fluctuations. In 1472, sailors from Portugal entered the Wouri River estuary and were amazed by the abundance of shrimp; they named it Rio dos Camarões, from which Cameroon got its name.

Portuguese settlers were followed by the Dutch and later by the Germans. The local inhabitants put up a stiff resistance to German penetration. At the beginning of World War I, Allied troops ousted the Germans, and in 1919, the French and the British partitioned the colony. The eastern part, covering 80 percent of the territory, went to the French, and the western part went to the British. Henceforth, each of the two powers made its mark on Cameroon; the French opting for a policy of assimilation and the British adopting indirect rule.

When the winds of nationalism began to blow across Africa after World War II, the two colonies expressed a desire to be reunited. Ahmadou Ahidjo proclaimed the French zone independent on January 1, 1960, and reunification of the colonies took effect in 1961. Cameroon became a united republic in 1972, the Republic of Cameroon in 1983, and it now has a presidential system of government.

The current government encourages development and a free market economy. The number of state-owned industries that have been privatized in the last several years has increased significantly. During the past decade, a fledgling free press has also been established. Cameroon's infrastructure, though not up to a developed nation's standards, is better than the infrastructures of its neighbors.

Government

Cameroon is a republic comprised of 10 regions made up of 58 administrative divisions. The legal system is based on French civil law with a common-law influence. Cameroon has a multiparty system and has had two presidents since independence: Ahmadou Ahidjo (January 1, 1960–November 4, 1982) and Paul Biya (November 6, 1982–present). President Biya was re-elected to a fourth term in 2011.

Cameroon is part of the drive for political reform and democracy sweeping the African continent. Over the past decade, the transition to a democratic form of government has been marked by intermittent civil unrest and a continuing national debate on the future of the country. Peace Corps staff continually monitors the political situation to keep Volunteers informed.

Economy

The economy grew from independence in 1960–85. In 1986, prospects darkened due to the collapse of world prices for Cameroon's major export commodities and poor management of state funds. Since then, Cameroon has seen a shrinking economy and serious money shortages. The declining economic situation has led to a substantial increase in crime.

As in many African countries, income disparities are wide and corruption is endemic. The state is still the biggest employer. Privatization efforts underway in Cameroon are making significant improvements in services to the general population.

Agriculture is the mainstay of Cameroon's economy, providing a living for 80 percent of the population and accounting for one-third of gross domestic product and half of all export earnings. It is one of the few net food exporters in Africa. While Cameroon is currently self-sufficient in food production, there is concern that this trend is not sustainable.

In 2006, Cameroon reached the "achievement point" in its negotiations with the International Monetary Fund and other donors. This "achievement" relieved the country of more than $300 million in debt, which may now be used for development purposes.

People and Culture

Cameroon is a crossroads where many of the human and cultural features of sub-Saharan Africa are present. Its population is a mosaic of approximately 300 ethnic groups of Bantu, Sudanese, and Arab origins. The largest ethnic groups are the Bamiléké of the west, the Béti and Bassa of the south, and the Fulbé and Massa of the north.

There are 239 languages spoken in Cameroon, including English, French, and pidgin. Both French and English are official languages. Of the total population of approximately 20 million, about 80 percent live in the French-speaking eastern part of the country and 20 percent live in the formerly British western part.

Approximately 50 percent of the population is considered to be animist, 30 percent Christian, and the remainder Muslim. The largest Muslim concentration is in northern Cameroon. Despite its great tribal, linguistic, and religious diversity, Cameroon has made considerable progress toward integration and national unity.

Environment

Cameroon is an elongated, triangular country situated at the juncture of West and Equatorial Africa. It extends from the Gulf of Guinea to Lake Chad and is a land of physical, climatic, and cultural contrasts. Cameroon has been called an "Africa in miniature" because of all the variations—from desert to rain forest to grassland plateau to mountains to tropical beaches—in its geography. Dense forest and heavy rainfall cover the south, including the capital of Yaoundé. The western provinces feature a mountain range with steep slopes and a prolonged rainy season. A vast grassland plateau covers the north.

RESOURCES FOR FURTHER INFORMATION

Following is a list of websites for additional information about the Peace Corps, Cameroon, and to connect you to returned Volunteers and other invitees. Please keep in mind that although we try to make sure all these links are active and current, we cannot guarantee it. If you do not have access to the Internet, visit your local library. Libraries offer free Internet usage and often let you print information to take home.

A note of caution: As you surf the Internet, be aware that you may find bulletin boards and chat rooms in which people are free to express opinions about the Peace Corps based on their own experience, including comments by those who were unhappy with their choice to serve in the Peace Corps. These opinions are not those of the Peace Corps or the U.S. government, and we hope you will keep in mind that no two people experience their service in the same way.

General Information About Cameroon

www.countrywatch.com

On this site, you can learn anything from what time it is in the capital of Cameroon to how to convert from the dollar to the Cameroonian currency. Just click on Cameroon and go from there.

www.lonelyplanet.com/destinations

Visit this site for general travel advice about almost any country in the world.

www.state.gov

The State Department's website issues background notes periodically about countries around the world. Find Cameroon and learn more about its social and political history. You can also go to the site's international travel section to check on conditions that may affect your safety.

www.psr.keele.ac.uk/official.htm

This includes links to all the official sites for governments worldwide.

www.geography.about.com/library/maps/blindex.htm

This online world atlas includes maps and geographical information, and each country page contains links to other sites, such as the Library of Congress, that contain comprehensive historical, social, and political background.

www.cyberschoolbus.un.org/infonation/info.asp

This United Nations site allows you to search for statistical information for member states of the U.N.

www.worldinformation.com

This site provides an additional source of current and historical information about countries around the world.

Connect With Returned Volunteers and Other Invitees

www.rpcv.org

This is the site of the National Peace Corps Association, made up of returned Volunteers. On this site you can find links to all the Web pages of the "Friends of" groups for most countries of service, comprised of former Volunteers who served in those countries. There are also regional groups that frequently get together for social events and local volunteer activities. Or go straight to the Friends of Cameroon site: www.friendsofcameroon.org.

www.PeaceCorpsWorldwide.org

This site is hosted by a group of returned Volunteer writers. It is a monthly online publication of essays and Volunteer accounts of their Peace Corps service.

Online Articles/Current News Sites About Cameroon

http://hmnet.com/africa/1africa.html

Site of the Africa Information Center

http://allafrica.com/cameroon/

Cameroon news site

www.irinnews.org/Africa-Country.aspx?Country=CM

Cameroon news site

www.afrol.com/countries/cameroon

Cameroon news site

www.cia.gov/library/publications/the-world-factbook/geos/cm.html

CIA Factbook on Cameroon

In addition, BBC News, VOA news, International Herald Tribune, and RFI (Radio France Internationale) all have good news websites on Africa.

Recommended Books

- Ardener, Edwin. *Kingdom on Mount Cameroon: Studies in the History of the Cameroon Coast 1500–1960*. New York: Berghahn Books, 1996.

- Barley, Nigel. *The Innocent Anthropologist: Notes From a Mud Hut*. Prospect Heights, Ill.: Waveland Press, 2000.

- Delancey, Mark. *Cameroon: Dependence and Independence*. Boulder, Colo.: Westview Press, 1989.

- Goheen, Miriam. *Men Own the Field, Women Own the Crops: Gender and Power in the Cameroon Grassfields*. Madison: University of Wisconsin Press, 1996.

- Smith, Mary-Ann Tirone. *Lament for a Silver-Eyed Woman*. New York: William Morrow, 1987.

Books About the History of the Peace Corps

- Hoffman, Elizabeth Cobbs. *All You Need is Love: The Peace Corps and the Spirit of the 1960s*. Cambridge, Mass.: Harvard University Press, 2000.

- Rice, Gerald T. *The Bold Experiment: JFK's Peace Corps*. Notre Dame, Ind.: University of Notre Dame Press, 1985.

- Stossel, Scott. *Sarge: The Life and Times of Sargent Shriver*. Washington, D.C.: Smithsonian Institution Press, 2004.

- Meisler, Stanley. *When the World Calls: The Inside Story of the Peace Corps and its First 50 Years*. Boston, Mass.: Beacon Press, 2011.

Books on the Volunteer Experience

- Dirlam, Sharon. *Beyond Siberia: Two Years in a Forgotten Place*. Santa Barbara, Calif.: McSeas Books, 2004.

- Casebolt, Marjorie DeMoss. *Margarita: A Guatemalan Peace Corps Experience*. Gig Harbor, Wash.: Red Apple Publishing, 2000.

- Erdman, Sarah. Nine Hills to Nambonkaha: Two Years in the Heart of an African Village. New York, N.Y.: Picador, 2003.

- Hessler, Peter. *River Town: Two Years on the Yangtze*. New York, N.Y.: Perennial, 2001.

- Kennedy, Geraldine ed. *From the Center of the Earth: Stories out of the Peace Corps*. Santa Monica, Calif.: Clover Park Press, 1991.

- Thompsen, Moritz. *Living Poor: A Peace Corps Chronicle*. Seattle, Wash.: University of Washington Press, 1997 (reprint).

LIVING CONDITIONS AND
VOLUNTEER LIFESTYLE

Communications
Mail

Few countries in the world offer the level of mail service considered normal in the United States. Mail takes a minimum of two to three weeks to arrive and may take up to six weeks. Some mail may simply not arrive, or may arrive with clipped edges because a postal worker has tried to see if any money was inside. The vast majority of letters arrive in decent time. Advise your family and friends to number their letters for tracking purposes and to include "Airmail" and "Par Avion" on their envelopes.

During pre-service training (your first eight weeks in Cameroon), letters and packages should be sent to:

> "Your name"
> Peace Corps Trainee
> Corps de la Paix
> B.P. 215
> Yaoundé, Cameroon

Once you have finished training and are at your site, letters can continue to be sent to the address above or you may tell family and friends to send mail directly to your new address at your site.

Telephones

Cellular telephones are popular in Cameroon and can easily be purchased in all major cities for less than $40. They do not function in all areas of the country, but service is spreading rapidly. Most trainees purchase a cell phone shortly after arrival in Cameroon (cellular telephones from the United States will not work in Cameroon unless they are GSM phones).

In the event of a serious problem, Peace Corps/Cameroon will notify the Office of Special Services (OSS) at the Peace Corps headquarters in Washington, D.C., which will then contact your family. Advise your family members that in the case of a family emergency, they should contact the OSS at 855.855.1961 ext. 1470. The line is staffed 24 hours a day, including weekends and holidays. The direct number is 202.692.1470.

Computer, Internet, and Email Access

Internet is widely available throughout Cameroon. However, the connection speed is quite slow and unreliable. Many Volunteers will only have intermittent access to the Internet.

At the Peace Corps office in Yaoundé, Volunteers have access to computers with high-speed Internet connections. Many Volunteers brings laptop computers to Cameroon. If you do, you may spend a lot of time worrying about your equipment in transport and at home (not to mention the hassle of lugging it around), and parts may not be available. The choice is up to you. Peace Corps/Cameroon is unable to provide technical support to Volunteers who choose to bring a computer, and will not reimburse you for any needed repairs. Computers and other high-value items also heighten your exposure to opportunistic theft. Make sure to have any high-value items insured as the Peace Corps will not reimburse for loss or theft.

Housing and Site Location

During training, you will live with a Cameroonian family. After training, you are likely to have your own house in the community where you are posted. Volunteers are assigned to sites throughout Cameroon, which range in size from large cities to small villages. Your assignment will depend on the project, host country needs, housing availability, and your preferences. Cameroon's development needs are the first priority in posting Volunteers.

Arrangements for housing are made by the Peace Corps and depend on resources available in the community. You will have to be flexible in your housing expectations. The Peace Corps tries to ensure that Volunteers have lodging that allows for independence and privacy. Your house may have walls made of concrete or mud bricks and most likely a tin roof. A typical Volunteer house has a sitting room, a bedroom, and a cooking area. Some houses have inside toilets/shower areas, while others have nearby pit latrines. Nearly one-half of all Volunteers have electricity, but running water is not common. Both electricity and running water are unreliable everywhere in Cameroon. Peace Corps/Cameroon provides an all-terrain bicycle and a helmet, a mosquito net, and a water filter. Upon your swearing in as a Volunteer, the Peace Corps will give you a modest settling-in allowance to purchase household necessities and furniture.

Some sites are very isolated (more than 50 kilometers from the next Volunteer), and travel can sometimes be difficult due to the poor quality of roads and infrequent public transportation (50 kilometers can take anywhere from three to eight hours of travel time, depending on road conditions). Other posts are short distances from one another and are near paved roads.

Living Allowance and Money Management

The local currency is the CFA franc (XAF). Online currency converters can provide the current exchange rate for the U.S. dollar. Volunteers receive a monthly living allowance of

160,000 CFA to cover their cost of living simply, but adequately, while serving in Cameroon. The living allowance covers the cost of utilities, domestic help, household supplies, clothing, food, work-related transport and supplies, and modest entertainment and recreation expenditures. Housing is provided at no cost. In addition to a living allowance, you will receive $24 each month as a vacation allowance. If you are requested by the Peace Corps to travel, you will be given additional money for transportation and lodging.

Volunteers should open a bank account that is easily accessible from their site, and the living allowance will be deposited monthly into the account. Although credit cards can be used in large hotels in Yaoundé and Douala, they can rarely be used elsewhere in Cameroon. ATMs that use the Plus network exist in nearly all regional capitals and large towns. Identity theft, however, can be a problem in Cameroon, and an additional reason to use caution when using credit, debit, or ATM cards in the country. For vacation travel outside of Cameroon, a credit card may be useful. Many Volunteers bring extra cash, which can be exchanged for a fee at banks, for emergencies and vacation travel. A safe is available in the Peace Corps office for use by Volunteers. Note that the Peace Corps is not able to transfer personal funds from the United States to a Volunteer or trainee.

Food and Diet

If there is one country on the African continent that can be described as a land of plenty, Cameroon certainly deserves the title. Cameroon is the breadbasket for this region, and local foods such as millet, plantains, beans, cassava, coco yams, sweet potatoes, and okra, together with meats, fish, poultry, and seasonal fruits and vegetables, provide the bulk of the diet. However, food availability varies significantly by region: in the south and west of the country, a wide range of vegetables and fruits are always available. In the more arid north, variety is far more limited. Meats, fish, and poultry are generally available everywhere. Some of the villages in which Volunteers are posted have a weekly market, and others must depend on a neighboring market for various items. Some canned and imported Western foods and products will be available in towns where you live or in the larger regional capitals, but they are expensive. Being a vegetarian should not pose a problem. However, the stricter you are in a vegetarian diet, the more challenging it will be. Cameroon's climate is generally favorable for vegetable gardening, and many Volunteers supplement what is available at the market with their own harvest. Spices are among the few items not available in Cameroon, so you may want to bring some with you.

Transportation

Volunteers use trains, buses, bush taxis, motorcycle taxis, bikes, and occasionally planes. Public transportation in Cameroon is relatively reliable. A train runs to the Grand North each day. Bus routes run between Yaoundé, Douala, Bafoussam, Bamenda, and other major towns. Planes however, are often late, have limited routes, and are frequently canceled.

Taxis are available and inexpensive in most major towns. Motorcycle taxis are common in the Grand North regions and are becoming more common elsewhere in the country. Finally, minivans or "bush taxis" traverse both paved and unpaved roads, bringing passengers and their belongings (including bunches of bananas, goats, pigs, etc.) to all but the tiniest villages.

Although available, travel is not always easy. Due to a lack of road maintenance and the fact that some major routes have yet to be paved, transportation can be difficult and time-consuming—especially in the rainy season. Since the transport infrastructure is limited, every means is used to its fullest capacity. This can mean squeezing six or more people into a city taxi or bush taxi or sharing seats on the train.

You may have to rely on public transport to travel to major towns to do banking, mail letters, use the Internet, etc. In doing this, you must take an active role in choosing the safest, most reliable transport. This means refusing to enter vehicles that are poorly maintained or driven by irresponsible chauffeurs and waiting for the next car.

Geography and Climate

Cameroon is a land of geographic and climatic diversity, with desert, rain forest, savanna, ancient and active volcanoes, and tropical beaches. The climate ranges from extremely hot and dry in the north, to cool in the central plateau, to humid and hot in the south.

It is best to bring clothing that will work in all of these regions, as you will not know in advance where you will be posted. Clothing—new, used, and custom-made—is widely available in Cameroon, the latter at very inexpensive prices, so you can have many of your clothes made locally.

Social Activities

Forming relationships with members of your community will be challenging and gratifying. Cameroonians are hospitable and generous, and their extended family structure makes for an open-door policy and a welcoming attitude to visitors. Demonstrating an interest in the local culture will greatly increase the integration process and help you establish credibility as a member of the community. You will find that your acceptance into the community will depend a great deal on your willingness to experience the Cameroonian lifestyle. The most satisfied Volunteers integrate into their communities while maintaining a good sense of who they are. They eat local food, speak the local language, and attend important village ceremonies such as baptisms, funerals, and marriages.

Drinking alcohol is often a part of the social fabric in many regions of Cameroon, which sometimes can create a more aggressive living or working environment. Although Volunteers are encouraged to socialize with Cameroonians and participate in ceremonies and festivities as a means of learning about the culture, it is advisable that drinking in public be limited to special occasions and after work hours. Volunteers need to be aware of the messages they send during their daily interactions in the community.

Professionalism, Dress, and Behavior

One of the difficulties of finding your place as a Peace Corps Volunteer is fitting into the local culture while maintaining your own cultural identity and acting like a professional—all at the same time. It is not an easy thing to resolve. You will be working as a representative of a government ministry or a professional organization and, as such, you will be expected to dress and behave accordingly. Professional dress standards are high in Cameroon. Being neat and cleanly dressed is a sign of respect and pride.

A foreigner who wears dirty, unkempt, or old clothes is likely to be considered an affront. Trousers (for men and women in some regions), blouses/shirts, skirts (below the knee), and dresses are appropriate wear for work. If your dress is inappropriate (shorts, halter tops, short skirts, form-fitting or low-cut blouses, dirty or torn clothing), you may not be readily accepted in your job. For women, inappropriate dress and behavior will attract unwanted attention. Cameroonians are not likely to directly comment on your dress, but they are likely to think that you either do not know what is culturally acceptable or do not care. You should certainly bring at least one dressy outfit for important or ceremonial occasions.

The Peace Corps expects Volunteers to behave in a way that will foster respect within their community and reflect well on the Peace Corps and on citizens of the United States. You will receive an orientation to appropriate behavior and cultural sensitivity during pre-service training. As a Volunteer, you have the status of an invited guest, and you should be sensitive to the habits, tastes, and taboos of your hosts.

Personal Safety

More detailed information about the Peace Corps' approach to safety is contained in the "Health Care and Safety" chapter, but it is an important issue and cannot be overemphasized. As stated in the Volunteer Handbook, becoming a Peace Corps Volunteer entails certain safety risks. Living and traveling in an unfamiliar environment (oftentimes alone), having a limited understanding of local language and culture, and being perceived as well-off are some of the factors that can put a Volunteer at risk. Many Volunteers experience varying degrees of unwanted attention and harassment. Petty thefts and burglaries are not uncommon, and incidents of physical and sexual assault do occur, although most Cameroon Volunteers complete their two years of service without incident. The Peace Corps has established procedures and policies designed to help you reduce your risks and enhance your safety and security. These procedures and policies, in addition to safety training, will be provided once you arrive in Cameroon. Using these tools, you are expected to take responsibility for your safety and well-being.

Each staff member at the Peace Corps is committed to providing Volunteers with the support they need to successfully meet the challenges they will face to have a safe, healthy, and productive service. We encourage Volunteers and families to look at our safety and security information on the Peace Corps website at **www.peacecorps.gov/safety**.

Information on these pages gives messages on Volunteer health and Volunteer safety. There is a section titled "Safety and Security – Our Partnership." Among topics addressed are the risks of serving as a Volunteer, posts' safety support systems, and emergency planning and communications.

Rewards and Frustrations

You will certainly experience ups and downs during your time in Cameroon. One week, cultural and language differences will seem exotic, exciting, and inviting; the next week, you may see them as barriers to everything you want to experience and accomplish in Cameroon. You will need serious coping skills—humor, humility, and the ability to forge strong social connections—to get you through the difficult passes. You should expect hardship and difficulty to be part of your weekly routine and be aware that the Peace Corps staff will not always be there to help you through every cycle of ups and downs.

Particularly during the first year of service, many Volunteers feel very alone in their work because they lack the support one gets from working with people who share a common background. You may feel isolated by language and cultural barriers. Paradoxically, you also may feel that you are never alone, but are always on parade or under scrutiny. Even the few people who find this exhilarating at first eventually find it irritating and burdensome.

Your initial reaction to a new country is likely to be one of delight and curiosity, but working in a country is another matter. "Flexible time," where "soon" can mean anything from 20 minutes to the next day or week, can become very frustrating. Eventually you will learn to turn the burdens into tools in your work; combining your own cultural identity with the new culture, you will learn to both live comfortably and accomplish your objectives. Learning to function well in a community so vastly different from anything you have known in the United States is part of the challenge and magic of being a Peace Corps Volunteer.

It is not an exaggeration to state that every successful Peace Corps project begins by identifying a particular host country national who is competent, reliable, understanding, and dedicated. This can be a long, slow, arduous task requiring many months of frequently frustrated efforts. A deep conviction that you share a common humanity with your host that transcends the cultural differences will be a big help. In the end, these relationships are the ones that will add tremendous meaning to your time here.

One of the difficulties faced by some Volunteers is a lack of clarity of their role in development: to what extent are you an agent of change, and to what extent are you a respectful, conforming guest and fellow worker? The answer is not clear cut because both motivations are relevant, and yet they are clearly contradictory. Whether you teach or work in community development, you will encounter an established traditional system, some of which may seem absurd, grossly inefficient, pointless, or superstitious. Do you oppose it or go along with it? If you oppose it, you will encounter resistance and hostility—often subtle, sometimes blatant. On the other hand, if you go along with the system, nothing changes and you feel useless. Volunteers who follow the latter course often rationalize their passivity with statements like: "After all, we are not here to change things" or "Who is to say that the American way of life is any better than the host country's?" There is no easy solution. Most Volunteers work out a flexible approach in which sometimes they oppose the system and sometimes they go along with it, hopefully without giving up the objective of imparting something of themselves in the process.

While it is possible that you will sail through every stressful situation without encountering any discomfort, that would be unusual. There are times for all Volunteers when the difficult conditions under which they live and work prove upsetting. Many experience intense feelings of discouragement and futility, especially during the first year of service. Things that seemed clear become unclear. The best direction to take is obscured. You do not feel in control of a situation or a problem, and this can be frightening. These are the times when coping skills and your social support system are critical.

Having said all that, the rewards of Peace Corps service are immense. The very tangible rewards are the acquisition of language, technical, and cross-cultural skills that improve your ability to make your way anywhere in the world. In addition, your two years of overseas work experience gives you a significant advantage for future international work, as well as for many jobs based in the U.S. However, it is the intangible rewards that are most gratifying to Volunteers: the cross-cultural understanding you gain from integration into a community for a long period of time and the deep relationships that surely come of that. Even for the veteran world traveler, these experiences will be deeper and more profound than any other travel adventure you have had. You cannot help leaving the Peace Corps with a broader world view and a deeper understanding of the realities experienced by others around the globe. And you will never be under-stimulated by your environment. More importantly, while having this incredible experience, you will also have the profound satisfaction of making a difference to an individual, a community, and a country.

PEACE CORPS TRAINING

Pre-Service Training

Pre-service training lasts from eight to nine weeks, depending on the project, and follows a community-based training methodology. This means you will live in a Cameroonian village or town with a small group of other trainees and periodically come together in a common location for sessions with the members of your training class. While in training, you will conduct individual research and have formal language classes. Although pre-service training can be stressful as you try to learn new skills in a different and often confusing environment, a highly experienced training staff is available to help you.

Technical Training

Technical training will prepare you to work in Cameroon by building on the skills you already have and helping you develop new skills in a manner appropriate to the needs of the country. The Peace Corps staff, Cameroon experts, and current Volunteers will conduct the training program. Training places great emphasis on learning how to transfer the skills you have to the community in which you will serve as a Volunteer.

Technical training will include sessions on the general economic and political environment in Cameroon and strategies for working within such a framework. You will review your technical sector's goals and will meet with the Cameroon agencies and organizations that invited the Peace Corps to assist them. You will be supported and evaluated throughout the training to build the confidence and skills you need to undertake your project activities and be a productive member of your community.

Language Training

As a Peace Corps Volunteer, you will find that language skills are key to personal and professional satisfaction during your service. These skills are critical to your job performance, they help you integrate into your community, and they can ease your personal adaptation to the new surroundings. Therefore, language training is at the heart of the training program. You must successfully meet minimum language requirements to complete training and become a Volunteer. Cameroon language instructors teach formal language classes five days a week in small groups of four to five people.

Your language training will incorporate a community-based approach. In addition to classroom time, you will be given assignments to work on outside of the classroom and with your host family. The goal is to get you to a point of basic social communication skills so you can practice and develop language skills further once you are at your site. Prior to being sworn in as a Volunteer, you will work on strategies to continue language studies during your service.

Cross-Cultural Training

As part of your pre-service training, you will live with a Cameroon host family. This experience is designed to ease your transition to life at your site. Families go through an orientation conducted by Peace Corps staff to explain the purpose of pre-service training and to assist them in helping you adapt to living in Cameroon. Many Volunteers form strong and lasting friendships with their host families.

Cross-cultural and community development training will help you improve your communication skills and understand your role as a facilitator of development. You will be exposed to topics such as community mobilization, conflict resolution, gender and development, nonformal and adult education strategies, and political structures.

Health Training

During pre-service training, you will be given basic medical training and information. You will be expected to practice preventive health care and to take responsibility for your own health by adhering to all medical policies. Trainees are required to attend all medical sessions. The topics include preventive health measures and minor and major medical issues that you might encounter while in Cameroon. Nutrition, mental health, setting up a safe living compound, and how to avoid HIV/AIDS and other sexually transmitted diseases (STDs) are also covered.

Safety Training

During the safety training sessions, you will learn how to adopt a lifestyle that reduces your risks at home, at work, and during your travels. You will also learn appropriate, effective strategies for coping with unwanted attention and about your individual responsibility for promoting safety throughout your service.

Additional Trainings During Volunteer Service

In its commitment to institutionalize quality training, the Peace Corps has implemented a training system that provides Volunteers with continual opportunities to examine their commitment to Peace Corps service while increasing their technical and cross-cultural skills. During service, there are usually three training events. The titles and objectives for those trainings are as follows:

- In-service training: Provides an opportunity for Volunteers to upgrade their technical, language, and project development skills while sharing their experiences and reaffirming their commitment after having served for three to six months.

- Midterm conference (done in conjunction with technical sector in-service): Assists Volunteers in reviewing their first year, reassessing their personal and project objectives, and planning for their second year of service.

- Close-of-service conference: Prepares Volunteers for the future after Peace Corps service and reviews their respective projects and personal experiences.

The number, length, and design of these trainings are adapted to country-specific needs and conditions. The key to the training system is that training events are integrated and interrelated, from the pre-departure orientation through the end of your service, and are planned, implemented, and evaluated cooperatively by the training staff, Peace Corps staff, and Volunteers.

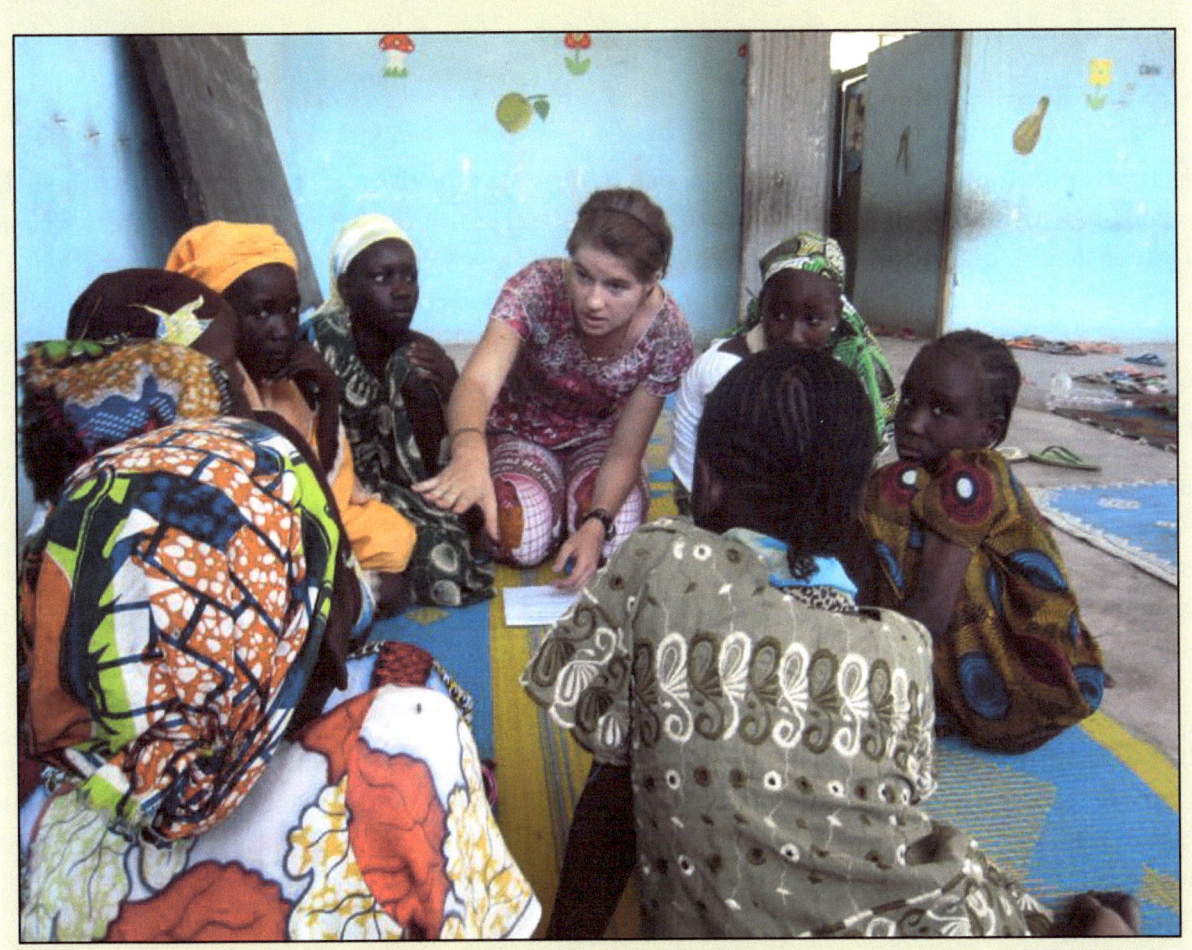

YOUR HEALTH CARE AND SAFETY IN CAMEROON

The Peace Corps' highest priority is maintaining the good health and safety of every Volunteer. Peace Corps medical programs emphasize the preventive, rather than the curative, approach to disease. The Peace Corps in Cameroon maintains a clinic with a full-time medical officer, who takes care of Volunteers' primary health care needs. Additional medical services, such as testing and basic treatment, are also available in Cameroon at local hospitals. If you become seriously ill, you will be transported either to an American-standard medical facility in the region or to the United States.

Health Issues in Cameroon

Volunteer failing to take preventive measures to stay healthy. The most common health problems in Cameroon are minor ones that are also found in the United States. These include colds, diarrhea, constipation, sinus infections, skin infections, headaches, dental problems, minor injuries, sexually transmitted infections, emotional problems, and alcohol abuse. These problems may be more frequent or compounded by life in Cameroon because certain environmental factors raise the risk or exacerbate the severity of illness and injuries.

Many illnesses that afflict Volunteers worldwide are entirely preventable if proper food and water precautions are taken. These illnesses include food poisoning, parasitic infections, hepatitis A, dysentery, Guinea worms, tapeworms, and typhoid fever. Your medical officer will discuss specific standards for water and food preparation in Cameroon during pre-service training.

The most common major health concerns in Cameroon are malaria, amoebic dysentery, hepatitis, HIV/AIDS, schistosomiasis, and filariasis. Because malaria is endemic in Cameroon, taking anti-malarial medication is mandatory. You will be vaccinated against hepatitis A and B, meningitis A and C, tetanus/diphtheria, typhoid, and rabies. Thoroughly washing fruits and vegetables and boiling your drinking water can prevent amoebic dysentery. You will be tested for schistosomiasis, a parasitic disease, at the end of service.

It is critical to your health that you promptly report to the Peace Corps health unit for scheduled immunizations and that you let your medical officer know immediately of significant illnesses and injuries.

Helping You Stay Healthy

The Peace Corps will provide you with all the necessary inoculations, medications, and information to stay healthy. Upon your arrival in Cameroon, you will receive a medical handbook. At the end of training, you will receive a medical kit with supplies to take care of mild illnesses and first aid needs. The contents of the kit are listed later in this chapter.

During pre-service training, you will have access to basic medical supplies through the medical officer. However, you will be responsible for your own supply of prescription drugs and any other specific medical supplies you require, as the Peace Corps will not order these items during training. Please bring a three-month supply of any prescription drugs you use, since they may not be available here and it may take several months for shipments to arrive.

You will have physicals at midservice and at the end of your service. If you develop a serious medical problem during your service, the medical officer in Cameroon will consult with the Office of Medical Services in Washington, D.C. If it is determined that your condition cannot be treated in Cameroon, you may be sent out of the country for further evaluation and care.

Maintaining Your Health

As a Volunteer, you must accept considerable responsibility for your own health. Proper precautions will significantly reduce your risk of serious illness or injury. The adage "An ounce of prevention ..." becomes extremely important in areas where diagnostic and treatment facilities are not up to the standards of the United States. The most important of your responsibilities in Cameroon is to take the following preventive measures:

Malaria. You will be serving in an area where malaria, a mosquito-borne disease, is prevalent. To suppress malaria, you must take an approved anti-malarial drug.You must continue taking prophylaxis throughout your service and for four weeks after you leave a malarial area. Keep in mind that no single or combined malaria prophylactic regimen is 100 percent effective. Avoidance of mosquito bites is imperative! By using bed nets, wearing appropriate clothing, and applying insect repellent to exposed skin, you will greatly reduce your risk of exposure to mosquito bites. Malaria can be effectively treated when prompt medical attention is sought but may be rapidly fatal if left untreated. Unfortunately, Volunteers who do not fully comply with Peace Corps recommendations occasionally contract malaria. You will be administratively separated if you refuse to take malaria prophylaxis.

Rabies. Rabies is present in Cameroon and in most other Peace Corps countries. Any possible exposure to a rabid animal must be reported immediately to the health unit. Rabies exposure can occur through animal bites, scratches from animals' teeth, and contact with animal saliva. Your medical officer will take into consideration many factors to decide the appropriate course of therapy necessary to prevent rabies. Rabies, if contracted, can be fatal. Peace Corps medical officers will provide all necessary rabies immunizations.

Injectable medications and immunizations. Injectable medications should be avoided unless given at the Peace Corps health unit or at a facility approved by your Peace Corps medical officer. There are risks of contacting HIV, hepatitis C, and other diseases if the equipment is not new and disposable. All immunizations are given at the Peace Corps health unit or at another Peace Corps-designated facility. If you sustain a wound, a local facility might want to give you an immunization against tetanus. You will be fully immunized against tetanus at the start of your service for a period of at least five years, so immunization at an in-country clinic is unnecessary and potentially dangerous (some tetanus immunizations can cause serious allergic reactions). If in doubt about your need for a tetanus booster, contact your medical officer.

HIV and other sexually transmitted infections. HIV is prevalent in Cameroon and increasing. Other STIs, such as herpes, gonorrhea, and syphilis, are also common. Abstinence is the only certain choice for prevention of HIV and other STIs. You are taking risks if you choose to be sexually active. To reduce risk, use a condom every time you have sex. Whether your partner is a host country citizen, a fellow Volunteer, or anyone else, do not assume this person is free of HIV/AIDS or other STIs. You should not assume that any sexual partner (fellow Volunteer, Cameroonian, or anyone else) has been practicing safe sex in Cameroon; even longer-term relationships in Cameroon require adequate protection and constant vigilance in terms of safe sex. Volunteers are highly encouraged to use condoms throughout Peace Corps service, even after testing and even in a long-term relationship. You will receive more information from your medical officer about this important issue.

Diarrheal illnesses. Diarrhea affects most Volunteers at some time during their service. Most cases are due to amoebas, giardia, or bacteria. These organisms are spread by consumption of contaminated food and water and are therefore preventable. A simple stool test helps the medical officer determine the cause of a case of diarrhea. You will be offered appropriate treatment following guidelines set by the Office of Health Services.

Viral hepatitis. Hepatitis A and B are both endemic in Cameroon. Hepatitis A is highly infectious and spreads through the fecal-oral route. Hepatitis B is transmitted by exposure to blood and bodily fluids, primarily through sexual contact. All Volunteers are vaccinated against hepatitis A and B while in Cameroon.

Dust. Dust is a problem during the dry season in Cameroon. It can produce chronic nasal congestion or watery nasal discharge. It can also lead to difficulty in breathing (wheezing) and watery, itchy eyes. If you have asthma, even if it is inactive, the dust, pollen, and molds in the atmosphere in Cameroon may exacerbate your symptoms. Breathing difficulties caused by allergies to dust or pollen may show up as wheezing or a dry, nonproductive cough during the night or after exercise. Volunteers with no history of asthma have developed wheezing in Cameroon. Allergies developed in-country will probably be resolved when you return to the United States, but it is still necessary to find out if there is an infectious cause for the difficulties and to treat any wheezing before the problem becomes severe.

Tuberculosis. Tuberculosis is a highly contagious, chronic bacterial disease that is widespread in Cameroon, and is spread by the sputum particles of individuals with open lung tuberculosis. Although your chances of contracting tuberculosis in Cameroon are small, you will have screening tests for tuberculosis during midservice and close-of-service exams.

Birth control. Volunteers are expected to adhere to an effective means of birth control to prevent an unplanned pregnancy. Your medical officer can help you decide on the most appropriate method to suit your individual needs. Contraceptive methods are available without charge from the medical officer.

Your medical officer will present other appropriate preventive measures Volunteers are expected to comply with and therapies recommended by the Peace Corps health unit or referral facility. It is critical to your health that you promptly report to the medical office or other designated facility for scheduled immunizations, and that you let the medical officer know immediately of significant illnesses and injuries.

Many illnesses that afflict Volunteers worldwide are entirely preventable if proper food and water precautions are taken. These illnesses include food poisoning, parasitic infections, hepatitis A, dysentery, Guinea worms, tapeworms, and typhoid fever. Your medical officer will discuss specific standards for water and food preparation in Cameroon during pre-service training.

Abstinence is the only certain choice for preventing infection with HIV and other sexually transmitted diseases. You are taking risks if you choose to be sexually active. To lessen risk, use a condom every time you have sex. Whether your partner is a host country citizen, a fellow Volunteer, or anyone else, do not assume this person is free of HIV/AIDS or other STDs. You will receive more information from the medical officer about this important issue.

Volunteers are expected to adhere to an effective means of birth control to prevent an unplanned pregnancy. Your medical officer can help you decide on the most appropriate method to suit your individual needs. Contraceptive methods are available without charge from the medical officer.

It is critical to your health that you promptly report to the medical office or other designated facility for scheduled immunizations, and that you let the medical officer know immediately of significant illnesses and injuries.

Women's Health Information

Pregnancy is treated in the same manner as other Volunteer health conditions that require medical attention but also have programmatic ramifications. The Peace Corps is responsible for determining the medical risk and the availability of appropriate medical care if the Volunteer remains in-country. Given the circumstances under which Volunteers live and work in Peace Corps countries, it is rare that the Peace Corps' medical and programmatic standards for continued service during pregnancy can be met.

If feminine hygiene products are not available for you to purchase on the local market, the Peace Corps medical officer in Cameroon will provide them. If you require a specific product, please bring a three-month supply with you.

Your Peace Corps Medical Kit

The Peace Corps medical officer will provide you with a kit that contains basic items necessary to prevent and treat illnesses that may occur during service. Kit items can be periodically restocked at the medical office.

Medical Kit Contents

Ace bandages
Adhesive tape
American Red Cross First Aid & Safety Handbook
Antacid tablets (Tums)
Antibiotic ointment (Bacitracin/Neomycin/ Polymycin B)
Antiseptic antimicrobial skin cleaner (Hibiclens)
Band-Aids
Butterfly closures
Calamine lotion
Cepacol lozenges
Condoms

Dental floss
Diphenhydramine HCL 25 mg (Benadryl)
Insect repellent stick (Cutter's)
Iodine tablets (for water purification)
Lip balm (Chapstick)
Oral rehydration salts
Oral thermometer (Fahrenheit)
Pseudoephedrine HCL 30 mg (Sudafed)
Robitussin-DM lozenges (for cough)
Scissors
Sterile gauze pads
Tetrahydrozaline eyedrops (Visine)
Tinactin (antifungal cream)
Tweezers

Before You Leave: A Medical Checklist

If there has been any change in your health – physical, mental, or dental – since you submitted your examination reports to the Peace Corps, you must immediately notify the Office of Medical Services. Failure to disclose new illnesses, injuries, allergies, or pregnancy can endanger your health and may jeopardize your eligibility to serve.

If your dental exam was done more than a year ago, or if your physical exam is more than two years old, contact the Office of Medical Services to find out whether you need to update your records. If your dentist or Peace Corps dental consultant has recommended that you undergo dental treatment or repair, you must complete that work and make sure your dentist sends requested confirmation reports or X-rays to the Office of Medical Services.

If you wish to avoid having duplicate vaccinations, contact your physician's office to obtain a copy of your immunization record and bring it to your pre-departure orientation. If you have any immunizations prior to Peace Corps service, the Peace Corps cannot reimburse you for the cost. The Peace Corps will provide all the immunizations necessary for your overseas assignment, either at your pre-departure orientation or shortly after you arrive in Cameroon. You do not need to begin taking malaria medication prior to departure.

Bring a three-month supply of any prescription or over-the-counter medication you use on a regular basis, including birth control pills. Although the Peace Corps cannot reimburse you for this three-month supply, it will order refills during your service. While awaiting shipment – which can take several months – you will be dependent on your own medication supply. The Peace Corps will not pay for herbal or nonprescribed medications, such as St. John's wort, glucosamine, selenium, or antioxidant supplements.

You are encouraged to bring copies of medical prescriptions signed by your physician. This is not a requirement, but they might come in handy if you are questioned in transit about carrying a three-month supply of prescription drugs.

If you wear eyeglasses, bring two pairs with you – a pair and a spare. If a pair breaks, the Peace Corps will replace them, using the information your doctor in the United States provided on the eyeglasses form during your examination. The Peace Corps discourages you from using contact lenses during your service to reduce your risk of developing a serious infection or other eye disease. Most Peace Corps countries do not have appropriate water and sanitation to support eye care with the use of contact lenses. The Peace Corps will not supply or replace contact lenses or associated solutions unless an ophthalmologist has recommended their use for a specific medical condition and the Peace Corps' Office of Medical Services has given approval.

If you are eligible for Medicare, are over 50 years of age, or have a health condition that may restrict your future participation in health care plans, you may wish to consult an insurance specialist about unique coverage needs before your departure. The Peace Corps will provide all necessary health care from the time you leave for your pre-departure orientation until you complete your service. When you finish, you will be entitled to the post-service health care benefits described in the Peace Corps Volunteer Handbook. You may wish to consider keeping an existing health plan in effect during your service if you think age or pre-existing conditions might prevent you from re-enrolling in your current plan when you return home.

SAFETY AND SECURITY:
OUR PARTNERSHIP

Serving as a Volunteer overseas entails certain safety and security risks. Living and traveling in an unfamiliar environment, a limited understanding of the local language and culture, and the perception of being a wealthy American are some of the factors that can put a Volunteer at risk. Property theft and burglaries are not uncommon. Incidents of physical and sexual assault do occur, although almost all Volunteers complete their two years of service without serious personal safety problems.

Beyond knowing that Peace Corps approaches safety and security as a partnership with you, it might be helpful to see how this partnership works. Peace Corps has policies, procedures, and training in place to promote your safety. We depend on you to follow those policies and to put into practice what you have learned. An example of how this works in practice – in this case to help manage the risk of burglary – is:

- Peace Corps assesses the security environment where you will live and work
- Peace Corps inspects the house where you will live according to established security criteria
- Peace Corps provides you with resources to take measures such as installing new locks
- Peace Corps ensures you are welcomed by host country authorities in your new community
- Peace Corps responds to security concerns that you raise
- You lock your doors and windows
- You adopt a lifestyle appropriate to the community where you live
- You get to know neighbors
- You decide if purchasing personal articles insurance is appropriate for you
- You don't change residences before being authorized by Peace Corps
- You communicate concerns that you have to Peace Corps staff

Factors that Contribute to Volunteer Risk

There are several factors that can heighten a Volunteer's risk, many of which are within the Volunteer's control. By far the most common crime that Volunteers experience is theft. Thefts often occur when Volunteers are away from their sites, in crowded locations (such as markets or on public transportation), and when leaving items unattended.

Before you depart for Cameroon there are several measures you can take to reduce your risk:

- Leave valuable objects in the U.S.
- Leave copies of important documents and account numbers with someone you trust in the U.S.
- Purchase a hidden money pouch or "dummy" wallet as a decoy
- Purchase personal articles insurance

After you arrive in Cameroon, you will receive more detailed information about common crimes, factors that contribute to Volunteer risk, and local strategies to reduce that risk. For example, Volunteers in Cameroon learn to:

- Choose safe routes and times for travel, and travel with someone trusted by the community whenever possible
- Make sure one's personal appearance is respectful of local customs
- Avoid high-crime areas
- Know the local language to get help in an emergency
- Make friends with local people who are respected in the community
- Limit alcohol consumption

As you can see from this list, you must be willing to work hard and adapt your lifestyle to minimize the potential for being a target for crime. As with anywhere in the world, crime does exist in Cameroon. You can reduce your risk by avoiding situations that place you at risk and by taking precautions. Crime at the village or town level is less frequent than in the large cities; people know each other and generally are less likely to steal from their neighbors. Tourist attractions in large towns are favorite worksites for pickpockets.

The following are other security concerns in Cameroon of which you should be aware:

When it comes to your safety and security in the Peace Corps, you have to be willing to adapt your behavior and lifestyle to minimize the potential for being a target of crime. As with anywhere in the world, crime does exist in Cameroon. You can reduce your risk by avoiding situations that make you feel uncomfortable and by taking precautions. Crime at the village or town level is less frequent than in the large cities: people know each other and generally will not steal from their neighbors. Tourist attractions in large towns, for instance, are favorite worksites for pickpockets. The following are safety concerns in Cameroon of which you should be aware:

Vehicle accidents are the single greatest risk to your safety in Cameroon. Volunteers are strongly encouraged to wear seat belts whenever available and to avoid riding in overcrowded public buses or vans. Because of the poor and dangerous conditions of roads in the interior of the country and the speed at which vehicles travel, Peace Corps/Cameroon has established a transportation policy that limits Volunteer travel to Yaoundé and the provincial capitals.

The homes of some Volunteers have been burglarized in the past, and Volunteers will need to take the same precautions that they would take in the United States. The Peace Corps advises on proper home safety during training, including installation of deadbolt locks and other safety features in Volunteer homes.

In recent years, street crime has drastically increased in Cameroon, and a number of Volunteers have been victims. By far, the most common incidents are petty thefts and burglary. Many of these incidents have taken place in regional capitals. There has also been an increase in violent crime where weapons are involved (also in urban areas). Carjacking, particularly in Yaoundé and Douala, has also been reported. In rural areas, there is usually less crime; however, in some regions of the country there are incidents of road banditry.

Volunteers are required to wear a protective helmet whenever riding on a two-wheeled motorized vehicle or a bicycle. Failure to comply with this regulation will result in immediate administrative separation from the Peace Corps and you will be sent home. There is no appeal.

Physical and sexual assault occurs in Peace Corps countries worldwide, just as it does in the United States. You can avoid some of the risk by changing your own behavior. You will receive a thorough briefing on how to minimize this risk in Cameroon. If harassment or assault occurs, the safety and security coordinator, APCDs, and PCMOs are available to assist you. It is important that you report any incident(s) to the duty officers (medical or emergency) and receive appropriate care, including care for your emotional well-being. Medications are available to reduce your risk of pregnancy and infection with HIV after sexual contact, so it is important to contact the health unit immediately. The Peace Corps can also advise you about your options for prosecuting an attacker. While whistles and exclamations may be fairly common on the street, this behavior can be reduced if you dress conservatively, abide by local cultural norms, and respond according to the training you will receive.

While whistles and exclamations may be fairly common on the street, this behavior can be reduced if you dress conservatively, abide by local cultural norms, and respond according to the training you will receive.

Staying Safe: Don't Be a Target for Crime

You must be prepared to take on a large degree of responsibility for your own safety. You can make yourself less of a target, ensure that your home is secure, and develop relationships in your community that will make you an unlikely victim of crime. While the factors that contribute to your risk in Cameroon may be different, in many ways you can do what you would do if you moved to a new city anywhere: Be cautious, check things out, ask questions, learn about your neighborhood, know where the more risky locations are, use common sense, and be aware. You can reduce your vulnerability to crime by integrating into your community, learning the local language, acting responsibly, and abiding by Peace Corps policies and procedures. Serving safely and effectively in Cameroon will require that you accept some restrictions on your current lifestyle.

Support from Staff

If a trainee or Volunteer is the victim of a safety incident, Peace Corps staff is prepared to provide support. All Peace Corps posts have procedures in place to respond to incidents of crime committed against Volunteers. The first priority for all posts in the aftermath of an incident is to ensure the Volunteer is safe and receiving medical treatment as needed. After assuring the safety of the Volunteer, Peace Corps staff response may include reassessing the Volunteer's worksite and housing arrangements and making any adjustments, as needed. In some cases, the nature of the incident may necessitate a site or housing transfer. Peace Corps staff will also assist Volunteers with preserving their rights to pursue legal sanctions against the perpetrators of the crime. It is very important that Volunteers report incidents as they occur, not only to protect their peer Volunteers, but also to preserve the future right to prosecute. Should Volunteers decide later in the process that they want to proceed with the prosecution of their assailant, this option may no longer exist if the evidence of the event has not been preserved at the time of the incident.

Crime Data for Cameroon

Crime data and statistics for Cameroon, which is updated yearly, are available at the following link: **http://www.peacecorps.gov/countrydata/Cameroon**. Please take the time to review this important information.

Few Peace Corps Volunteers are victims of serious crimes and crimes that do occur overseas are investigated and prosecuted by local authorities through the local courts system. If you are the victim of a crime, you will decide if you wish to pursue prosecution. If you decide to prosecute, Peace Corps will be there to assist you. One of our tasks is to ensure you are fully informed of your options and understand how the local legal process works. Peace Corps will help you ensure your rights are protected to the fullest extent possible under the laws of the country.

If you are the victim of a serious crime, you will learn how to get to a safe location as quickly as possible and contact your Peace Corps office. It's important that you notify Peace Corps as soon as you can so Peace Corps can provide you with the help you need.

Volunteer Safety Support in Cameroon

The Peace Corps' approach to safety is a five-pronged plan to help you stay safe during your service and includes the following: information sharing, Volunteer training, site selection criteria, a detailed emergency action plan, and protocols for addressing safety and security incidents. Cameroon's in-country safety program is outlined below.

The Peace Corps/Cameroon office will keep you informed of any issues that may impact Volunteer safety through **information sharing**. Regular updates will be provided in Volunteer newsletters and in memorandums from the country director. In the event of a critical situation or emergency, you will be contacted through the emergency communication network. An important component of the capacity of Peace Corps to keep you informed is your buy-in to the partnership concept with the Peace Corps staff. It is expected that you will do your part in ensuring that Peace Corps staff members are kept apprised of your movements in-country so they are able to inform you.

Volunteer training will include sessions on specific safety and security issues in Cameroon. This training will prepare you to adopt a culturally appropriate lifestyle and exercise judgment that promotes safety and reduces risk in your home, at work, and while traveling. Safety training is offered throughout service and is integrated into the language, cross-cultural aspects, health, and other components of training. You will be expected to successfully complete all training competencies in a variety of areas, including safety and security, as a condition of service.

Certain **site selection criteria** are used to determine safe housing for Volunteers before their arrival. The Peace Corps staff works closely with host communities and counterpart agencies to help prepare them for a Volunteer's arrival and to establish expectations of their respective roles in supporting the Volunteer. Each site is inspected before the Volunteer's arrival to ensure placement in appropriate, safe, and secure housing and worksites. Site selection is based, in part, on any relevant site history; access to medical, banking, postal, and other essential services; availability of communications, transportation, and markets; different housing options and living arrangements; and other Volunteer support needs.

You will also learn about Peace Corps/Cameroon's **detailed emergency action plan**, which is implemented in the event of civil or political unrest or a natural disaster. When you arrive at your site, you will complete and submit a site locator form with your address, contact information, and a map to your house. If there is a security threat, you will gather with other Volunteers in Cameroon at predetermined locations until the situation is resolved or the Peace Corps decides to evacuate.

Finally, in order for the Peace Corps to be fully responsive to the needs of Volunteers, it is imperative that Volunteers immediately report any security incident to the Peace Corps office. The Peace Corps has established protocols for **addressing safety and security**

incidents in a timely and appropriate manner, and it collects and evaluates safety and security data to track trends and develop strategies to minimize risks to future Volunteers.

DIVERSITY AND CROSS-CULTURAL ISSUES

In fulfilling its mandate to share the face of America with host countries, the Peace Corps is making special efforts to assure that all of America's richness is reflected in the Volunteer corps. More Americans of color are serving in today's Peace Corps than at any time in recent history. Differences in race, ethnic background, age, religion, and sexual orientation are expected and welcomed among our Volunteers. Part of the Peace Corps' mission is to help dispel any notion that Americans are all of one origin or race and to establish that each of us is as thoroughly American as the other despite our many differences.

Our diversity helps us accomplish that goal. In other ways, however, it poses challenges. In Cameroon, as in other Peace Corps host countries, Volunteers' behavior, lifestyle, background, and beliefs are judged in a cultural context very different from their own. Certain personal perspectives or characteristics commonly accepted in the United States may be quite uncommon, unacceptable, or even repressed in Cameroon.

Outside of Cameroon's capital, residents of rural communities have had relatively little direct exposure to other cultures, races, religions, and lifestyles. What people view as typical American behavior or norms may be a misconception, such as the belief that all Americans are rich and have blond hair and blue eyes. The people of Cameroon are justly known for their generous hospitality to foreigners; however, members of the community in which you will live may display a range of reactions to cultural differences that you present.

To ease the transition and adapt to life in Cameroon, you may need to make some temporary, yet fundamental compromises in how you present yourself as an American and as an individual. For example, female trainees and Volunteers may not be able to exercise the independence available to them in the United States; political discussions need to be handled with great care; and some of your personal beliefs may best remain undisclosed. You will need to develop techniques and personal strategies for coping with these and other limitations. The Peace Corps staff will lead diversity and sensitivity discussions during pre-service training and will be on call to provide support, but the challenge ultimately will be your own.

Overview of Diversity in Cameroon

The Peace Corps staff in Cameroon recognizes the adjustment issues that come with diversity and will endeavor to provide support and guidance. During pre-service training, several sessions will be held to discuss diversity and coping mechanisms. We look forward to having male and female Volunteers from a variety of races, ethnic groups, ages, religions, and sexual orientations, and hope that you will become part of a diverse group of Americans who take pride in supporting one another and demonstrating the richness of American culture.

What Might a Volunteer Face?

Possible Issues for Female Volunteers

Cameroon is a traditional patriarchal culture. Although there are sometimes women in positions of great influence in large cities and towns, the people of Cameroon in general have not had much experience with women who take on professional roles or who live independently of their families. Cameroonian male colleagues, supervisors, and acquaintances may make unwanted advances toward single women. This problem is less common for female Volunteers who have been accepted into their communities and who have built a network of female friends and counterparts. Learning to live and work constructively in the context of the differing status of women and men and standards of behavior (including sexual behavior) is probably the greatest challenge for female Volunteers in Cameroon. To address this issue, Peace Corps/Cameroon has a Volunteer/staff committee that works on important issues of girls' and women's empowerment.

Possible Issues for Volunteers of Color

Cameroonians may make some stereotypic assumptions about Volunteers of color. They may not believe that you are American, commenting that "you don't look American." African-American Volunteers may be treated as Cameroonians according to local norms (which can be positive and negative). They may be asked if there really are black people in America and may be called a white person in the local dialect. Asian-American Volunteers are often considered Chinese even when they have a different ethnic origin. They may also be assumed to be martial arts experts and asked to demonstrate their expertise. Children and others may call Asian Americans "heehaw," a mutation of *ni hao ma*, a greeting in Mandarin Chinese.

Possible Issues for Senior Volunteers

Older Volunteers are usually accorded respect, since Cameroonian culture recognizes that wisdom and life experience come with age. Older Volunteers may experience difficulty, however, in obtaining support from and mixing with younger Volunteers. In contrast, Volunteers in their early 20s may find that they have to make an extra effort to be accepted as professional colleagues, since Cameroonians of that age often are still pursuing education.

Possible Issues for Married Couple Volunteers

The shared experience of serving as a married couple is incredibly rewarding. Many of the challenges single Volunteers face are different or non-existent for couples. However, there are potential difficulties that married Volunteers can face. Married Volunteers are advised to establish a sense of individuality early on and do activities separately at their sites; otherwise, community members may not recognize their unique identities. When there are language proficiency differences between partners, it may be more difficult for the lower-level partner during the first few months of service. Married Volunteers who make an effort to be independent in their work and social aspects of service are most successful and most content with their work. Due to Cameroonian cultural and historical norms, women face unique discrimination that men do not. Among Volunteers, it is sometimes harder for married couples to be accepted into Volunteer social circles because their Volunteer experiences are perceived to be different. Despite such problems, the shared memories are a gift that will unite couples for the rest of their lives.

Possible Issues for Gay, Lesbian, or Bisexual Volunteers

Same-sex sexual acts are illegal in Cameroon and homosexuality is not publicly discussed or acknowledged except in very rare cases. Gay, lesbian, and bisexual Volunteers in Cameroon may feel that they have to hide their sexuality so as not to risk job effectiveness. In 2006, there was a major public crackdown on those believed to be participating in homosexual activity, and there have recently been several highly publicized cases of accused homosexuals being arrested. Dealing with constant questions about girlfriends or boyfriends, marriage, and children is something many Volunteers face on a regular basis. Forming a support network of gay, lesbian, or bisexual friends may be challenging but Peace Corps/Cameroon works to ensure a supportive, tolerant, and safe community for all Volunteers and staff.

A recommended resource for support and advice prior to and during your service is the Lesbian, Gay, Bisexual & Transgender U.S. Peace Corps Alumni website at **www.lgbrpcv.org**.

Possible Religious Issues for Volunteers

In general, Cameroonians are familiar with most Christian and Muslim traditions but have little familiarity with Judaism, Buddhism, Unitarianism, and other world religions. Cameroon, however, is an ethnically, religiously, and culturally diverse country and, as such, is tolerant of different religions. Cameroonians may not always agree with your beliefs, but it is unlikely that they will act negatively toward you because of them.

Possible Issues for Volunteers With Disabilities

As part of the medical clearance process, the Peace Corps Office of Medical Services determined that you were physically and emotionally capable, with or without reasonable accommodations, to perform a full tour of Volunteer service in Cameroon without unreasonable risk of harm to yourself or interruption of service. The Peace Corps/ Cameroon staff will work with disabled Volunteers to make reasonable accommodations for them in training, housing, jobsites, or other areas to enable them to serve safely and effectively.

While there is a large population of Cameroonians with disabilities, care and accommodation for these individuals are carried out informally and within the family or community. There is very little infrastructure to accommodate individuals with disabilities.

FREQUENTLY ASKED QUESTIONS

This list has been compiled by Volunteers serving in Cameroon and is based on their experience. Use it as an informal guide in making your own list, bearing in mind that each experience is individual. There is no perfect list! You obviously cannot bring everything on the list, so consider those items that make the most sense to you personally and professionally. You can always have things sent to you later. As you decide what to bring, keep in mind that you have a 100-pound weight limit on baggage. And remember, you can get almost everything you need in Cameroon.

How much luggage am I allowed to bring to Cameroon?

Most airlines have baggage size and weight limits and assess charges for transport of baggage that exceeds those limits. The Peace Corps has its own size and weight limits and will not pay the cost of transport for baggage that exceeds these limits. The Peace Corps' allowance is two checked pieces of luggage with combined dimensions of both pieces not to exceed 107 inches (length + width + height) and a carry-on bag with dimensions of no more than 45 inches. Checked baggage should not exceed 100 pounds total with a maximum weight of 50 pounds for any one bag.

Peace Corps Volunteers are not allowed to take pets, weapons, explosives, radio transmitters (shortwave radios are permitted), automobiles, or motorcycles to their overseas assignments. Do not pack flammable materials or liquids such as lighter fluid, cleaning solvents, hair spray, or aerosol containers. This is an important safety precaution.

What is the electric current in Cameroon?

In Cameroon, all appliances are powered with 220 volts. However, there may be large fluctuations in power, and most appliances should be protected with a voltage regulator. These can be purchased throughout Cameroon.

How much money should I bring?

Volunteers are expected to live at the same level as the people in their community. You will be given a settling-in allowance and a monthly living allowance, which should cover your expenses. Volunteers often wish to bring additional money for vacation travel to other countries. Credit cards and traveler's checks are preferable to cash. If you choose to bring extra money, bring the amount that will suit your own travel plans and needs.

When can I take vacation and have people visit me?

Each Volunteer accrues two vacation days per month of service (excluding training). Leave may not be taken during training, the first three months of service, or the last three months of service, except in conjunction with an authorized emergency leave. Family and friends are welcome to visit you after pre-service training and the first three months of service as long as their stay does not interfere with your work. Extended stays at your site are not encouraged and may require permission from your country director. The Peace Corps is not able to provide your visitors with visa, medical, or travel assistance.

Will my belongings be covered by insurance?

The Peace Corps does not provide insurance coverage for personal effects; Volunteers are ultimately responsible for the safekeeping of their personal belongings. However, you can purchase personal property insurance before you leave. If you wish, you may contact your own insurance company; additionally, insurance application forms will be provided, and we encourage you to consider them carefully. Volunteers should not ship or take valuable items overseas. Jewelry, watches, radios, cameras, and expensive appliances are subject to loss, theft, and breakage, and in many places, satisfactory maintenance and repair services are not available.

Do I need an international driver's license?

Volunteers in Cameroon do not need an international driver's license because they are prohibited from operating privately owned motorized vehicles. Most urban travel is by bus or taxi. Rural travel ranges from buses and minibuses to trucks, bicycles, and lots of walking. On very rare occasions, a Volunteer may be asked to drive a sponsor's vehicle, but this can occur only with prior written permission from the country director. Should this occur, the Volunteer may obtain a local driver's license. A U.S. driver's license will facilitate the process, so bring it with you just in case.

What should I bring as gifts for Cameroon friends and my host family?

This is not a requirement. A token of friendship is sufficient. Some gift suggestions include knickknacks for the house; pictures, books, or calendars of American scenes; souvenirs from your area; hard candies that will not melt or spoil; or photos to give away.

Where will my site assignment be when I finish training and how isolated will I be?

Peace Corps trainees are not assigned to individual sites until after they have completed pre-service training. This gives Peace Corps staff the opportunity to assess each trainee's technical and language skills prior to assigning sites, in addition to finalizing site selections with their ministry counterparts. If feasible, you may have the opportunity to provide input on your site preferences, including geographical location, distance from other Volunteers, and living conditions. However, keep in mind that many factors influence the site selection process and that the Peace Corps cannot guarantee placement where you would ideally like to be. Most Volunteers live in small towns or in rural villages and are usually within one hour from another Volunteer. Some sites require a 10- to 12-hour drive from the capital.

How can my family contact me in an emergency?

The Peace Corps' Office of Special Services (OSS) provides assistance in handling emergencies affecting trainees and Volunteers or their families. Before leaving the United States, instruct your family to notify the Office of Special Services immediately if an emergency arises, such as a serious illness or death of a family member. During normal business hours, the number for the Office of Special Services is 855.855.1961, then select option 2; or directly at 202-692-1470. After normal business hours and on weekends and holidays, the OSS duty officer can be reached at the above number. For non-emergency questions, your family can get information from your country desk staff at the Peace Corps by calling 855.855.1961.

Can I call home from Cameroon?

Yes. It is easy to dial the U.S. from a cell phone and it usually costs about $0.25 a minute. PCVs with adequate internet connections may also be able to Skype, but be aware that low bandwidth can make this difficult.

Should I bring a cellular phone with me?

You can bring a cell phone, but it will need to be a quad-band phone to work in Cameroon. Most phones in the U.S. are tri-band and won't work in Cameroon. You can buy phones in Cameroon very inexpensively ($20–$30) and most PCVs buy their phones upon arrival. Phones go through rough conditions in Cameroon and are frequently stolen. Consequently, you may want to forego bringing a nice phone.

Will there be email and Internet access?

Internet access is widely available in Cameroon, but the connection tends to be slow and unreliable. You may have to travel to have access to email so be prepared to live without it on a daily basis.

Should I bring my computer?

Like cell phones, computers suffer from the extreme conditions of humidity, heat, and dust. They are also susceptible to theft. However, the price of laptops and net books has decreased dramatically in the past few years, and you will likely find it very useful to have a computer for your work. Peace Corps regional offices often have wireless internet and, in this situation, you will be happy to have your own computer. You may want to consider personal article insurance in case of theft or loss.

WELCOME LETTERS FROM COUNTRY VOLUNTEERS

From a Health Volunteer:

Dear Incoming Volunteers,

Congratulations on your acceptance to Peace Corps/Cameroon! As I'm writing this, I've spent one year thus far in the southwest region of Cameroon. It's hardly possible how fast the time has gone for me. Integration, work, socializing, travel, and much-needed downtime will fill your schedule. The Peace Corps is a life-changing experience, not only because the website says it will be, but because you will learn so much about Cameroonian culture, develop a broader worldview, and, of course, fully understand what you are capable of. Getting through the application process is the first baby step of all there is to experience in Peace Corps/Cameroon.

Arriving in Cameroon was my first journey to Africa, and unforgettable. I was nervous and excited anticipating what the next two years of my life would look like. Upon arriving, our group met some current PCVs that gave me a new perspective on what was to come. Ask any PCV what they noticed about the current PCVs when they first arrived in-country. They will tell you there is an air about a PCV that every Peace Corps trainee envies. It's an air of confidence, of contentment, of understanding a new culture, and adopting it as one's own. I don't know at what point a PCV adopts this air, but it instantly became a quality I was prepared to strive for. I wanted to go home not only having completed two years' worth of work and integration, but to have that air of a wiser person for having had the Peace Corps experience.

You also, like I was one year ago, are about to embark on this journey. You will go through three months of training and, in that short time alone, learn so much about a new way of life. Life without running water and electricity, life without paved roads and toilets, life with large loving families and hand-sewn dresses, life with delicious new foods and outdoor kitchens, the list goes on. Then you will move to post and be adopted by an entire community.

I live in Nguti, a village of about 4,000 people in the southwest region of Cameroon. My village is an Anglophone region, although I speak pidgin to communicate with the majority of people. As a Health Volunteer, I have focused my work on maternal health and HIV/AIDS education and support. It is important to combine what your community needs with what you are happy doing. I found my own niche in HIV and maternal health. Currently, my main projects include teaching health lessons to mothers at a vaccination clinic each week, running an HIV support group that also does home visits together for those tested HIV-positive around the community, and teaching a training of trainers course to a group of adults on a variety of health topics. I have been making future plans to create a Prevention of Mother To Child Transmission (PMTCT) women's group, teach a training of trainers course to all of the teachers in Nguti schools, do a water sanitation project with a local NGO, and do an education tour for all of the surrounding bush villages. Finding work once you arrive at post may be a challenge, but once you get to know your community, understand their needs, and find the right people to work with, the work will pile up.

Cameroon is an incredibly welcoming and hospitable country. In my personal experience, people are happy to work and help their communities despite a cultural expectation of financial "motivation." You will have your share of ups and downs, but I've learned these are the things that give a PCV that air of confidence I so admire. You will learn things you'd never have considered before, see things that will make you laugh, cry, or just stop in your tracks for curiosity. I wish you luck and all the best. Enjoy every minute in Cameroon, the good and the bad. Culture shock is a roller coaster, but I promise this will be the best ride of your life if you let it!

—Katelyn Horberg

From a Community Economic Development Volunteer:

I'm a volunteer in a medium-sized city in the northwest of Cameroon. We have most comforts you could expect in Cameroon: I even have running water in the house most of the time. But the thing which matters most is taking in the experience, beautiful scenery, colorfully dressed people, the way things always seem chaotic but end up working out (after some time), fresh food doused in red palm oil, speaking in three or four different languages in one conversation and finally understanding it.

I'm wrapping up my service now, and more has happened in the last two years than I could have imagined and none of what happened was what I expected before I came. We say up here, don't have low or high expectations, but no expectations. Just adapt and be positive and you will have a wonderful experience.

As for work, I taught business classes in tiny credit unions without electricity, where most of my students didn't graduate high school. I worked with NGOs doing projects from poultry farming to donating textbooks to rural primary schools. Before I came to Cameroon, I was managing a restaurant in New York. Needless to say, not many skills cross over, but in training you realize how to manage work here. Training is long but be patient and use it as much as possible: it will help later on.

The best part of this entire experience for me has been getting integrated with my community. I truly feel at home here now as I type this listening to Nigerian gospel music (admittedly not my favorite) and watching motorcycle taxis whiz by the cafe I'm sitting in. As you come into this experience, know you can make out of it anything you want. You will have tons of freedom after training to pursue work that interests you; it's a wonderful opportunity to learn about the world and yourself.

—Jacob Iosso

From an Environment Volunteer:

As you have likely heard before, serving as an Environment Volunteer in Cameroon involves a variety of different experiences for different individuals. The position provides an incredible amount of autonomy and, as a result, the service is very much what you make it to be. You may have an area of expertise, such as agribusiness or environmental education, but working exclusively in one area the entire time does not seem to be the norm. This has certainly been my experience and I am currently involved in a variety of projects and cross-cultural activities.

One morning, I might lead a small workshop educating local farmers about composting techniques. Despite having had very little teaching experience in the United States, I've become quite confident giving presentations of this kind here in Cameroon. After overcoming the language barrier, I realized that in many instances, our communities have had very little exposure to these improved farming techniques and are eager to learn and experiment.

During the afternoon that follows, I might accompany a local man into the nearby city to observe the processing of his honey for market. While I never considered myself to be particularly business savvy back in the States, marketing tactics that seem obvious to me are occasionally completely foreign concepts to the farmers and businesses I collaborate with. I think that as Americans we have all been exposed to such a strong dose of commercialism that we have an innate sense of how product labels and advertisements should appear. On another afternoon I might trek down to the nursery my counterpart started and check on our tree seedlings. If it's a particularly rainy day I might just relax on my porch with a good book. As a Volunteer, each day is ours to occupy and it is up to us to seek out activities possessing the most potential for community development. The evening could bring dinner with a neighbor or a meal prepared at home. Afterward I might give computer lessons to one of the village boutique owners or help a high-school student with English homework.

Volunteer life can be challenging, simple, frustrating, gratifying, exhausting, and leisurely all at once. It is an incredibly unique opportunity to dive head first into the lifestyle and traditions of an utterly foreign culture while simultaneously working towards grassroots, bottom-up community development. Enjoy it! Welcome and good luck to you!

—Emily Olsen-Harbich

From an Education Volunteer:

Dear Future Volunteers,

My name is Justine Little and I am an Education Volunteer in the east region of Cameroon. I am in my second year of teaching in a public high school of about 500 students. My village has two other technical high schools, one of which is a private Catholic boarding school.

I live in Diang, a rural village 40 km outside of the regional capital, Bertoua. Because my school is small, I am one of two English teachers. I have taught the same classes both years: quatrième (equivalent to eighth grade), seconde (equivalent to 10th grade), and première (equivalent to 11th grade). My class size generally ranges from 40–80 students. My department colleague is on her second year of teaching, therefore she is not yet paid by the government so the PTA takes care of her, along with the other four unpaid but licensed teachers. We get along well, making collaborations a lot easier for both of us.

Most of the teachers do not permanently live in Diang because it is very small but its proximity to Bertoua makes it easy to commute. My colleagues are quite the dynamic group and are always brainstorming activities to keep a pleasant atmosphere among each other. We have a group called Amicale consisting of all the high-school administration and community members who are associated with the high school. We meet once a month at various Amicalists' homes to eat, drink, and socialize. The purpose of this group is to support one another and maintain a good relationship among each other.

Outside of teaching I coordinate two clubs: I have an English club and a girls' club. The English club helps students that are advanced in English to organize and practice activities that enable them to not only use their language skills but also help others who have difficulty and entertain during celebrations with songs, poems, and skits. My girls' club, officially named Club E.V.A. (Education de la Vie et a l'Amour), is a safe zone for girls to talk about personal concerns, spread awareness about HIV/AIDS, prevent unwanted pregnancies, and promote women's empowerment. I really enjoy working with these clubs because the students get an opportunity to let loose while still learning. Because of these relationships, I have been able to gain the trust and develop a strong cultural exchange between the students and myself.

Being an Education Volunteer has definitely been an unpredictable adventure. As a teacher, many of us expected our second year to be like the first, but nothing can really ever be the same. The truth is, there isn't really ever a dull moment. I have many memories since the day I set foot on Cameroonian soil and am excited for the new ones to come.

Good luck, future PCVs and welcome to Peace Corps/Cameroon!

—Justine Little

From a Youth in Development Volunteer

Dear soon-to-be Peace Corps/Cameroon volunteers, and even sooner-to-be Peace Corps/Cameroon trainees,

First of all: good call. The whole "signing up for the Peace Corps" thing. I don't think you'll regret it. If you're like me, you grew up with images from National Geographic and stories from family, friends, and neighbors who have traveled, and you knew that someday, just maybe, living abroad would be "your thing." Whether you've already been around the block, tested the water with a little travel here and there, or even if this is your very first venture crossing into foreign territory, I truly believe that from the first day, you'll be glad for the opportunity the Peace Corps provides for you to discover, learn, and serve.

Get ready. And by that, I mean be mentally prepared to never feel fully ready for anything you experience for the next 27 months. But don't worry: There's a freedom in the strangeness of it all, the being away from home, the new foods, the new languages, the new climates, the new cultures, and a point will come when the weirdest feeling will be when a day goes by without a new "first." Your first meal with couscous (no, not the same thing as we have in the States). Your first bush taxi. Your first marriage proposal by a passing moto-taxi driver. Don't worry. If you aren't familiar with these terms, you will be.

A little snapshot of my life. I'm a Youth in Development Volunteer posted in a rural community called Diang that has been incredibly welcoming and supportive since day one. I'm in the forested part of the east region, where the climate is a little cooler and more humid than the savannah areas just a few dozen kilometers away. Diang boasts only a few thousand residents when school's in session, and my largest culture shock so far has been having the high profile of being one of two Americans and one of five "white" people (though we're not all Caucasian) in my arrondissement (district), in stark contrast with my anonymous, blend-in-to-the-crowd city life back home in Springfield, Missouri.

The culture in this area is heavily Catholic, with a good number of Protestants and Muslims. People are generally very liberal regarding dress, and I've been outnumbered by jeans and tees on some days that I've chosen to wear Cameroonian traditional fabrics. Diang has a woman for a mayor, and we have electricity about 40–60 percent of the time, depending on the season. No running water, but the deep pumps provide me with clean, safe water. My diet is heavy in eggs and beans, and I go out of my way to work in the vegetables and fruits. There's no lack of meat, depending on how you feel about eating everything from deer and hare to porcupine, hedgehog, jungle cat, pangolin, monkey, toucan, viper, lizard, and a handful of other animals that we Americans see more often as cartoon animals than as supper.

I work with a couple of host organizations: one is an association of teachers (mostly primary-school principals) that was created to identify and help the most vulnerable children (mostly orphans) in our arrondissement. I work with the teachers to go into schools to teach things like sexual and reproductive health, good communication skills, and self-esteem to kids ages 11–16. The other association is made of young adults in a neighboring village who decided that they wanted to plant a communal field to sell produce and use the revenue to fund the school fees and materials for the children in their village. I also coordinate a girls' club at the local technical high school.

As you can imagine, work keeps me good and busy, but the pace of life is great. Living in the calm of the countryside helps me stay balanced, and I'm proud to say that much of my free time goes into spending time with my Cameroonian friends in village, having coffee or cooking with my post mate, and the occasional moto-taxi ride into the regional capital, 40 km away, where I can stock up on fresh veggies, dairy products, and manufactured goods that aren't always available in my village. I stay active, whether it's bike riding through the forest and fields, playing soccer or handball with the local health club, or just indulging in a little yoga on my veranda, looking out over the expanse of vegetation that grows behind my house for miles. I've also somehow evolved into quite a diligent housekeeper, thanks to my flexible schedule and the equal diligence of the critters of various shapes and sizes that wander into my territory (though I'm glad to say that nothing dangerous has scuttled in yet!).

Nowhere is perfect—I do get sick of having to explain why I'm not interested in eating monkey or marrying so-and-so's brother—but I am in love with my community, and the good outweighs the bad multifold. Soon, you'll be here to see firsthand, and my best advice is that you shouldn't let the little stuff freak you out. You'll get a few weeks in and already feel proud of how much you've learned, and the process doesn't slow down, but only deepens as you move from training into post.

I genuinely wish you the best as you make your preparations to come, and we'll be eagerly awaiting your arrival to the Peace Corps/Cameroon family, which, at over 200 people, is almost as large as the typical Cameroonian family. Almost. Speaking of which, don't forget to bring pictures! Hard-copy pictures from home—places you've lived, people you love, scenery, everything. You'll make friends fast telling Cameroonians about where you come from, and the photos last a lot longer than a Nature Valley bar, anyway.

—Laura Pearson

PACKING LIST

This list has been compiled by Volunteers serving in Cameroon and is based on their experience. Use it as an informal guide in making your own list, bearing in mind that each experience is individual. There is no perfect list! You obviously cannot bring everything on the list, so consider those items that make the most sense to you personally and professionally. You can always have things sent to you later. As you decide what to bring, keep in mind that you have an 100-pound weight limit on baggage. And remember, you can get almost everything you need in Cameroon.

General Clothing

- Professional clothes, slacks, button-up shirts, including blouses and skirts for women (you should have business casual clothing)

- Casual clothes for informal and after-work occasions

- Pictures of clothes you might want to have made (clothing patterns or photos from catalogs or magazines)

- Good-quality cotton shirts in dark colors (the dust in the air during the dry season and the sediment in the water year-round quickly cause light-colored clothing to become permanently discolored)

- Plenty of good-quality underwear, boxers, socks, and bras

- Sweater

- Rain jacket

- Two more formal outfits (female teachers, especially, should bring several nice-looking dresses they can wear in the classroom until they can have some clothes made in-country)

- Durable jacket (i.e., jean jacket or fleece)

- Shorts

- Bathing suit or swimming trunks

- Hats or baseball caps

Shoes

- One pair of comfortable dress shoes
- One pair of sandals for general use (e.g., Tevas or Chacos) and another pair for work
- One pair of running shoes
- One good-quality pair of work or hiking boots (especially Agriculture Volunteers)
- Waterproofing lotion for leather boots (if you bring boots)

Personal Hygiene and Toiletry Items

- Antibacterial wipes or hand sanitizers (useful when traveling)
- Any vitamin supplements or herbal remedies you take other than multivitamins, which may be provided by the Peace Corps
- Items that smell good, like lotions, incense, soaps, and sachets
- A three-month supply of all prescription drugs you are currently taking
- Two pairs of prescription eyeglasses (if you wear them) and repair kit
- Sunglasses
- Hair clips and ties
- Initial supply of toiletries (if you have favorite brands, bring enough to last two years)
- Sanitary pads (the Peace Corps usually supplies tampons, but they may not always be the size you want)
- Hair-cutting scissors
- Makeup and nail polish (hard to find locally and expensive)

Kitchen

- Measuring cups and spoons
- Plastic storage containers and zip-top-style bags of assorted sizes (large containers are good for organizing items such as medicine and clothing)
- Good kitchen knife and knife sharpener (if you're attached to a certain kind or quality)
- Swiss Army knife or Leatherman tool (very important to many Volunteers)
- Favorite recipe book
- Packaged mixes (sauces, salad dressings, soups, drink mixes such as Crystal Light or Gatorade)
- Favorite spices
- A variety of open-pollinated (recyclable) vegetable seeds, if you like to garden

Miscellaneous

- 12 passport-size photos (make sure to have them in hand when you arrive; Peace Corps/Cameroon will need them the day after you arrive for in-country documents)
- Anything that will make you happy and feel at home (personal touches)
- Map of Africa and/or Cameroon (those available here are expensive)
- Travel-size games, such as Yahtzee, Scrabble, and Uno, as well as playing cards
- Art supplies (paints, brushes, paper, colored pens, and crayons)
- Books (each Peace Corps satellite office has a library, but classics are hard to come by)
- A favorite writing utensil, with replacements or refills
- Stationery and an assortment of greeting cards

- U.S. stamps (returning Volunteers can take mail home for you)
- Addresses of people you may want to write
- IPod or other MP3 player (with speakers)
- External hard drive with music, recent TV shows or movies
- Digital reader such as a Kindle or Nook
- Weekend-sized backpack
- Bandannas
- Extra absorbent "swimmer's" micro-fiber towel (small and great for traveling)
- Sleeping bag (good for overnight stays at other Volunteers' homes)
- Bicycle shorts and gloves (a helmet, repair tools, and an under-seat bag are provided by the Peace Corps)
- Heavy-duty duct tape (good for everything)
- Compact flashlight (e.g., Maglite)
- Concealable money pouch or belt
- Water bottle (e.g. Nalgene or Sigg)
- Rechargeable batteries and battery charger
- Reliable watch (durable, water-resistant, inexpensive)
- Travel alarm clock
- Combination padlocks
- Good-quality portable umbrella
- High-school grammar books and literary anthologies (for English teachers)

PRE-DEPARTURE CHECKLIST

The following list consists of suggestions for you to consider as you prepare to live outside the United States for two years. Not all items will be relevant to everyone, and the list does not include everything you should make arrangements for.

Family

- Notify family that they can call the Peace Corps' Counseling and Outreach Unit at any time if there is a critical illness or death of a family member (24-hour telephone number: 1-855-855-1961, then press 2; or directly at 202-692-1470).

- Give the Peace Corps' On the Home Front handbook to family and friends.

Passport/Travel

- Forward to the Peace Corps travel office all paperwork for the Peace Corps passport and visas.

- Verify that your luggage meets the size and weight limits for international travel.

- Obtain a personal passport if you plan to travel after your service ends. (Your Peace Corps passport will expire three months after you finish your service, so if you plan to travel longer, you will need a regular passport.)

Medical/Health

- Complete any needed dental and medical work.

- If you wear glasses, bring two pairs.

- Arrange to bring a three-month supply of all medications (including birth control pills) you are currently taking.

Insurance

- Make arrangements to maintain life insurance coverage.

- Arrange to maintain supplemental health coverage while you are away. (Even though the Peace Corps is responsible for your health care during Peace Corps service overseas, it is advisable for people who have pre-existing conditions to arrange for the continuation of their supplemental health coverage. If there is a lapse in coverage, it is often difficult and expensive to be reinstated.)

- Arrange to continue Medicare coverage if applicable.

Personal Papers

- Bring a copy of your certificate of marriage or divorce.

Voting

- Register to vote in the state of your home of record. (Many state universities consider voting and payment of state taxes as evidence of residence in that state.)

- Obtain a voter registration card and take it with you overseas.

- Arrange to have an absentee ballot forwarded to you overseas.

Personal Effects

- Purchase personal property insurance to extend from the time you leave your home for service overseas until the time you complete your service and return to the United States.

Financial Management

- Keep a bank account in your name in the U.S.

- Obtain student loan deferment forms from the lender or loan service.

- Execute a Power of Attorney for the management of your property and business.

- Arrange for deductions from your readjustment allowance to pay alimony, child support, and other debts through the Office of Volunteer Financial Operations at 855.855.1961, extension 1770.

- Place all important papers—mortgages, deeds, stocks, and bonds—in a safe deposit box or with an attorney or other caretaker.